MW01097411

WHAT WAS LIFE LIKE UNDER APARTHEID?

HISTORY BOOKS FOR KIDS

Children's History Books

BABY PROFESSOR
EDUCATION KIDS

Speedy Publishing LLC
40 E. Main St. #1156
Newark, DE 19711
www.speedypublishing.com

In this book, we're going to talk about life under apartheid. So, let's get right to it!

THE AFRIKANERS GAIN POWER

In 1910, events happened in South Africa that brought about apartheid. Four South African British colonies banded together to form the Union of South Africa. Descendants of the original Dutch peoples who had come to the colonies began to gain a stronghold in the new government.

Map Showing Location of South Africa.

These Dutch descendants were called **Afrikaners.** As they gained more power, they wanted to deny rights to the black South Africans who were descendants of Africa's native tribes. They supported new laws that were based on keeping the black, native South Africans separate from the other populations.

Afrikaner Commandos.

These policies were called **Apartheid,** which means *"Apartness."* Apartheid laws were very harsh. They limited the rights of the black South Africans. They were not allowed to have certain types of jobs and they were not allowed to attend the schools of their choice. It placed restrictions on where they could live as well. Eventually, it took away most of their civil rights.

An Afrikander Wagon Transport in the Transvaal.

FOR USE BY WHITE PERSONS

THESE PUBLIC PREMISES AND THE AMENITIES THEREOF HAVE BEEN RESERVED FOR THE EXCLUSIVE USE OF WHITE PERSONS.

By Order Provincial Secretary

VIR GEBRUIK DEUR BLANKES

HIERDIE OPENBARE PERSEEL EN DIE GERIEWE DAARVAN IS VIR DIE UITSLUITLIKE GEBRUIK VAN BLANKES AANGEWYS.

Op Las Provinsiale Sekretaris

THE AFRIKANERS GAIN THE MAJORITY VOTE IN PARLIAMENT

The Afrikaners eventually became the most powerful political group and they were able to attain the majority vote in parliament in 1948. Apartheid became the official law of the land and divided up the population into four groups:

- **WHITES**, who received the best opportunities had the most rights

An old sign "For use by white persons" used after the forced removal of District Six inhabitants. Cape Town.

- **ASIANS,** who were generally from China or India were given fewer rights than whites

- **COLOREDS,** who were people of mixed race were given fewer rights than whites

- **BLACKS,** who were at the bottom of the society lost most of their rights

Hector Pieterson Memorial in Soweto, South Africa.

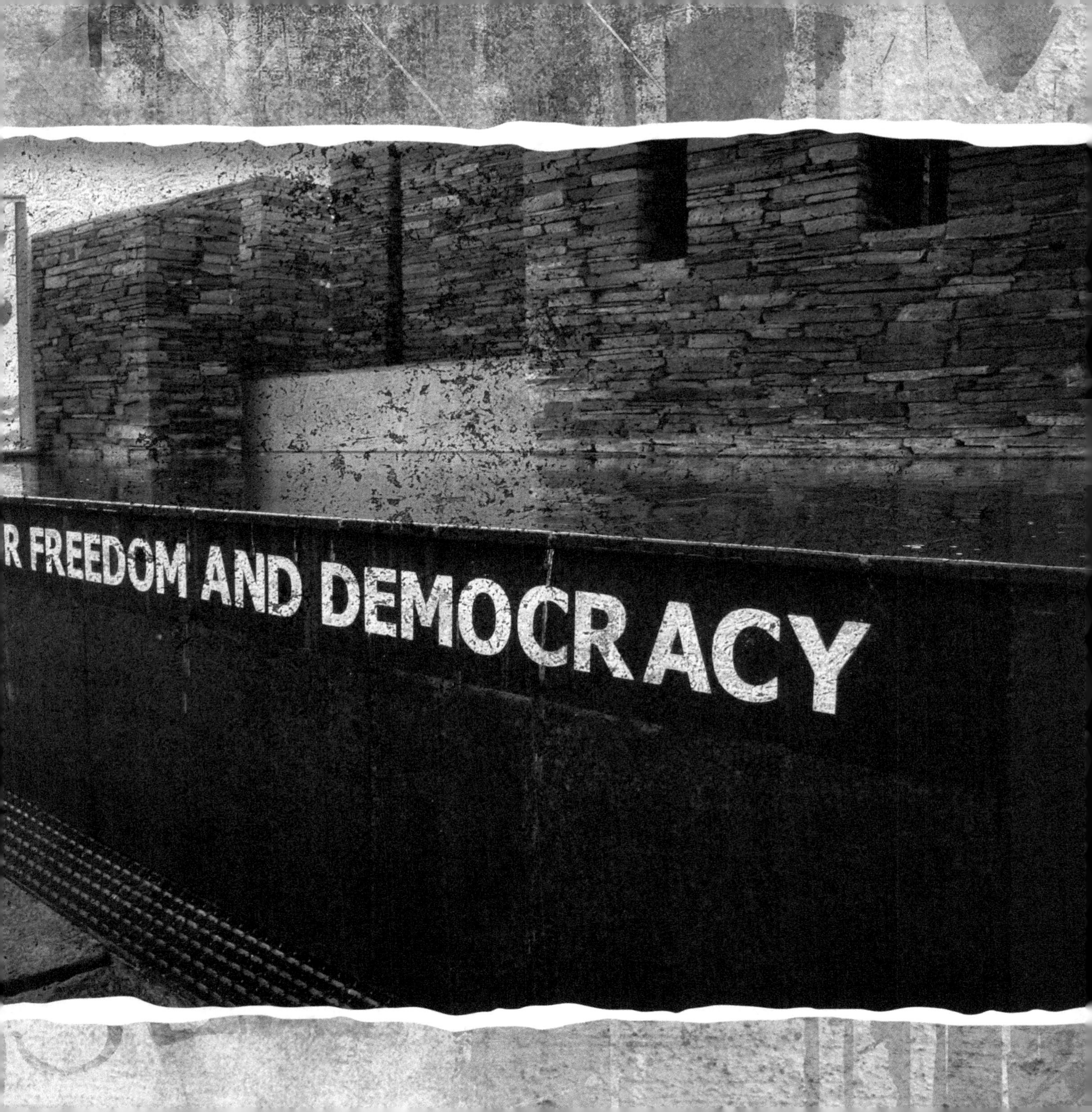
R FREEDOM AND DEMOCRACY

HOLD FAST
    TO DREAMS
FOR IF DREAMS DIE
LIFE IS A
    BROKEN-WINGED BIRD
THAT
    CANNOT FLY.

During apartheid, the Asians and Coloreds lived in segregated neighborhoods, separated from the whites. The black population lived in the most wretched conditions of all and received the poorest health care and jobs.

Cape Town: The street map of District Six with handwritten notes and poems from former residents on the floor.

Segregation had existed prior to 1948, but after the National Party, the political party of the Afrikaners, gained power, it became much worse. The areas in which whites could live and all others could not increased. These were the best urban areas and they had dwellings and businesses that were designated for *"whites only."*

Colored residents of Bonteheuwel township (Cape Town, South Africa).

The living areas for segregated Asians, Coloreds, and Blacks became smaller and impoverished. In 1950, the Group Areas Act was passed, which enforced the segregation of living spaces further.

Not everyone agreed with or went along with these horrible apartheid policies, but if they protested they were labeled as *"Communists"* and quickly thrown behind bars.

Bonteheuwel train station on the Cape Flats (Cape Town, South Africa).

HARDSHIPS DURING APARTHEID

During the time of apartheid, black South Africans struggled to find work to sustain themselves and their families. They took work in the mines and farms that were owned by whites. Sometimes they became servants. In the urban areas, they lived where they were completely segregated from the other populations. These township areas were basically slums. They had no indoor plumbing and the small houses were made of scraps.

Malan's Government in South Africa.

The provocative entrance to the Apartheid Museum in Cape Town, South Africa.

The government's system of separation was so rigid that it would actually have been hard for the police to enforce. To make sure people stayed where they belonged, they were given passes that designated their race and also stating where they lived as well as where they worked. If someone was caught without this pass, he or she was arrested and thrown behind bars.

The situation continued to get worse and worse. In the 1950s and 1960s, laws were added that prohibited any connection or conversation between whites and non-white races, except those who were in business relationships with the whites as employers and the non-whites as employees.

Township near Cape Town, South Africa.

ONLY

Just as was happening in the United States, transportation, restaurants, schools, and even drinking fountains and park benches were segregated, with areas that were set aside just for whites. The government of South Africa was trying to push the black people out of the country by stripping them of all their rights and creating intense hardship for them.

Apartheid bench in front of the High Court building explaining the race re-classification act of 1938. Cape Town, South Africa

LIVING IN THE BANTUSTAN

The population of native South Africans was four times the number of people in the white population. The white Afrikaners decided that these non-whites should only be allowed to vote for white government officials. In this way, the whites would be able to stay in power. They were able to pass these laws and gain the winning votes in parliament to put them into place.

KwaZulu was a bantustan in South Africa, intended by the apartheid government as a semi-independent homeland for the Zulu people.

However, they didn't stop there. They continued to put laws into place to strip all native black South Africans of their rights. They reasoned that If native black South Africans weren't citizens any more, then the government could treat them as if they were illegal aliens.

Bantustan in South Africa

One of the worst laws that was passed was the Homeland Act, which passed in 1951. This law formed areas of land that were reservations for the black South Africans. These homelands, called the Bantustan, were

KwaZulu was a bantustan in South Africa.

far from the rich urban areas where the white population lived. The native Africans were given the worst farming land where there were almost no natural resources.

Blacks living in the Bantustan areas had to work on farms that could barely provide enough for them to eat. They sometimes worked on white-owned farms or in white-owned mines for pay that was extremely low. They were not allowed to strike to gain more power since striking was against the law.

Zululand rural houses, Bantustan KwaZulu.

Some black South Africans were allowed to work in white-owned businesses or dwellings in the urban area, mostly in service jobs as waiters, maids, or janitors. To ensure that they kept to the proper areas, they had to carry passes that only allowed them to travel within the city for a time span of 72 hours. If a black person was stopped and didn't have his pass, he would be arrested.

Soweto - South West Township in Johannesburg, South Africa. SOWETO is the most populous black urban residential area in the country.

This image was captured during protests against Apartheid in South Africa in the 1980s.

To ensure that future generations followed the same societal system, the Afrikaners passed the Bantu Education Act of 1953. This act placed black children in separate schools and kept the standards in these schools very low so they would not be able to get any other types of jobs except service jobs.

An South African flag on a grunge wooden background with a shadow overly for freedom.

Nelson Mandela, 1937.

NELSON MANDELA

Nelson Mandela was a black South African who became a lawyer in 1942. By 1950, Mandela had become an activist who fought tirelessly against apartheid laws and oppression. Two years into his career as an activist, he was elected to the African National Congress, called ANC for short. This organization's goal was to change the racist policies of the South African government. He was elected as deputy president and this gave him a platform for his work to get rid of apartheid.

Just as Martin Luther King, Jr. in the United States, he was inspired by Mahatma Gandhi, the leader who had fought for India's independence using nonviolent protests. Over the next decade, Mandela led the ANC using powerful speeches against the white government leaders and nonviolent, strategic protests.

Mahatma Gandhi.

However, as time went on, Mandela gave up hope that such tactics could solve the evils of apartheid. He felt that guerilla warfare, bombings, and sabotage would be necessary to rid the country of apartheid for good.

Metal sculpture of Nelson Mandela at the site where he was arrested in 1962 by the apartheid government.

Mandela was getting attention on the world stage for his actions, but now that he had turned his focus to military tactics, not everyone agreed with what he was doing. He was put on trial for treason, by the Afrikaners, but, at the end of that trial he was set free. However, in 1962, as he and his groups were organizing a string of bombings in areas where oppression had been particularly great, he was caught.

Late South African president Nelson Mandela smiles as he poses for a portrait

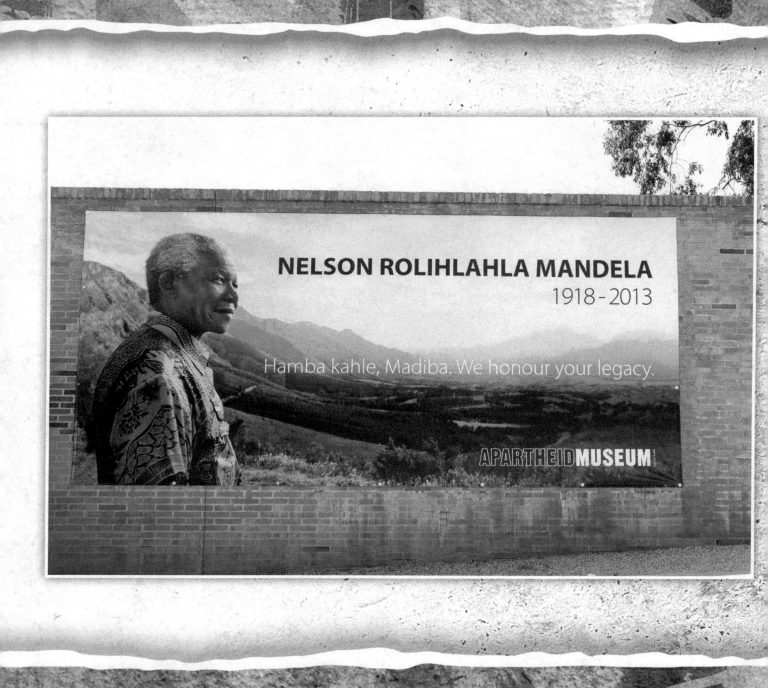

This level of violence was considered terrorism and it appeared that Mandela had aligned himself with some communist leaders, so information from United States agents from the CIA led to his capture and imprisonment by the South African government. He was sentenced to hard labor for a period of five years.

Nelson Mandela poster on the Apartheid Museum on August 21, 2014 in Johannesburg.

While he was in prison, he meditated about South Africa's situation. Over the next two decades, he was given many opportunities to be released if he denied his beliefs. Instead, he stayed in prison and became known as a freedom fighter who was willing to suffer for his beliefs and so that he could influence the needed reforms in South Africa.

Nelson Mandela mural in Williamsburg section in Brooklyn.

After Mandela had been behind bars for 23 years, he began to send letters to the Minister of Justice in the government. These handwritten letters sent by mail took several days to go back and forth. In this correspondence, the two men discussed how apartheid could be stopped. He was allowed a brief release from prison to have some needed surgery.

Prison cell of Nelson Mandela.

By 1990, Mandela had been imprisoned for 28 years. The government of the Union of South Africa was being pressured by groups both inside and outside the country to release this inspirational man. Once freed, Mandela became the president of the ANC where he immediately called for an end to violence throughout the country.

Solitary confinement cells in the old prison on Constitution Hill.

Outside Robben Island prison where Nobel Laureate and former President of South Africa Nelson Mandela was imprisoned.

Four years later, the government gave in to international pressure and held free elections. Mandela became the first black president of South Africa as a result of this free election. Many white people feared what would happen to them, but instead of persecuting them for their evil actions, Mandela created an atmosphere of putting these evils in the past so that the country could build a prosperous and free future.

Nelson Mandela imparted to the world his courage to fight and end Apartheid. He showed the world that everyone deserves fair treatment as he fought against oppression. With his death, we must always remember the values taught: these are justice, equality, fairness and peace for everyone.

Now you know more about life under apartheid. You can find more History books from Baby Professor by searching the website of your favorite book retailer.

Stop apartheid.

STOP APARTHEID

Printed in the USA
CPSIA information can be obtained
at www.ICGtesting.com
LVHW080259110823
754929LV00011B/370